TV NOW: Stars and Shows

Dorothy Scheuer

SCHOLASTIC INC.
New York Toronto London Auckland Sydney Tokyo

for David

Table of Contents

Grateful acknowledgment for their assistance in the preparation of this book is made to: ABC-TV, Alison Blank, CBS-TV, Stephen J. Cannell Productions, Dick Clark Productions, Epic Records, Laurence Frank & Company Public Relations, Janet Galen, Greg Holch, Alan Landsburg Productions, Roseanne Leto, Chip Lovitt, MGM/UA Television, MTM Enterprises, NBC-TV, Paramount Television, RCA, David Scheuer, The Shefrin Company, Debbie Thompson, 20th Century-Fox Television, Universal Television, Marcus Viscidi.

Photo research: Debbie Thompson

Scott Baio's Back and He's In Charge

As Chachi Arcola on *Happy Days*, **Scott Baio** spent the last eight years growing up right before our eyes. Now that he *is* grown up, he's taken over, as *Charles in Charge* (CBS). Scott plays a live-in family helper for the Pembroke family — an instant older brother to Jason (Michael Pearlman), Douglas (Jonathan Ward), and Lila (April Lerman).

Willie Aames is playing Charles' best friend, Buddy. That works out just fine, because Scott and Willie have been good buddies in real life for years. They worked together on the movie *Zapped!* and the TV series *We're Movin'*.

Scott got into show business when he was eight years old. "I watched TV a lot," he says. "I used to see little kids on the screen and say, 'Why can't I do that?' So I said, 'Ma, I want to do commercials.' And she said, 'Okay, you can try it.' "

Scott tried and succeeded. For a while it was fun. Then working got to be a drag. "Every day I'd come home from school and then have to go to another interview or audition," Scott says. "That was the only time I had to play. I got really mad one day and I said to my mother, 'Ma, I'm quitting.' "

He did, too. "Then, a year later, my manager called. He said, 'Listen, I know you don't want to work. But there's a role I think you might like and I think you're good for.' It just so happened it was raining that day and I had nothing to do. So I said okay. It was the movie *Bugsy Malone*. I went down and I read for it and got cast in it." He's been working steadily ever since.

Happy Days' producer Gary Marshall saw Scott in *Bugsy Malone*. He cast Scott in another series he was producing, called *Blansky's Beauties*. That show didn't last long. "But they were looking for a character to put into *Happy Days*," Scott says. Chachi Arcola was born.

Scott took time off from *Happy Days* to star in a spin-off with Erin Moran, called *Joanie Loves Chachi*. Unfortunately, the audience didn't love the series enough to keep it on the air. But everyone was happy when Erin and Scott returned to *Happy Days*. The love lasted, too. The characters were married in the series' final episode last spring.

There's a little bit of Scott in every part he plays, but he gets his inspiration from watching other people. "I try, not to imitate them, but to be like them and add something of myself," Scott says. Where does he find these people? "I think in every school they have every character you could ever want," he says. "When I hold a conversation with people, I'll watch how they act. I'll listen, but I'll also watch. Restaurants are good places for that."

Scott has found time to have a musical career. And his love for — and talent in — sports has won him a case full of trophies and great success on *Battle of the Network Stars* specials.

But Scott's main love is acting. He's starred in the movies *Foxes* and *Skatetown, U.S.A.*, and many TV specials. He's taken classes in comedy and learned one of the secrets of being a successful actor. "Three quarters of acting is listening," he says. "If you listen, you react to what the other person is saying. When you *really* listen, acting is easy."

Scott has his own apartment, but still spends most of his time with his parents and older brother and sister. He's 23 years old, and his birthday is September 22.

Mr. T. is on Everybody's A-Team

It's possible that you never saw *Rocky III* or *D.C. Cab*. It's possible — though hard to believe — that you've never seen *The A-Team* (NBC). But there can't be anyone in America who doesn't know who **Mr. T** is. You'd have to have been sound asleep for the last three years!

First of all, you can recognize Mr. T right away from the way he looks. From his Mandinkan haircut to his combat boots, Mr. T stands out. There's a method to his manner of dressing. The haircut is a symbol of his African roots. He wears mismatched socks on purpose. "A lot of poor kids don't have socks that go together," he says. "I make a joke of it so other kids won't make fun of them." The heavy gold jewelry around his neck stands for the African slaves who were brought to this country in chains. "I have turned those chains into gold," Mr. T says.

You can also recognize Mr. T by his attitude. (Maybe that's why they call him B.A. — Bad Attitude — on *The A-Team*.) He may look mean, but "Young people know I'm not," Mr. T says. "They wouldn't like me if I were."

Mr. T is visible proof that "tough" can mean "strong," but it doesn't have to mean "nasty."

Mr. T developed his strength while he was growing up in Chicago. His name was Lawrence Tureaud then. There were 12 brothers and sisters in his family. Lawrence was the youngest.

His father left when Lawrence was five. "My mother kept us together on $87 a month," Mr. T remembers. "We were the poorest people in the neighborhood. But we were happy. My mother taught us how to laugh and smile. She taught us how important it is to be the best we can at whatever we're doing."

When Lawrence grew up, he became a gym teacher. And he changed his name. "I got tired of people calling me 'boy,' " he says. "Now the first word out of anybody's mouth has to be 'Mister.' "

He got to be the best at what he was doing, too. Mr. T went from gym teacher to bodyguard. He made up to $5,000 a day protecting people like Leon Spinks, Michael Jackson, and Muhammad Ali.

Then he went to work as a bouncer in a Chicago disco. His job was to show troublemaking customers to the door. He entered a TV contest for "America's Toughest Bouncer" — and won a role in a movie.

Sylvester Stallone was looking for an actor to play tough Clubber Lang in *Rocky III*. His casting director happened to put on the TV the night of the "Toughest Bouncer" contest. "That's him!" she thought. The next stop for Mr. T was Hollywood.

In his movies and other appearances, Mr. T looks and acts pretty much the same as B.A. Baracas on *The A-Team*. There's a reason for this. "I think all the parts I play are me," he says. He doesn't mind that, but he'd still like to do other things. "I'd like to play one of Jesus' disciples," he says. "Maybe John the Baptist. Or, I'd like to play Moses."

His religion is important to Mr. T. "I can't hold a conversation without mentioning God," he says. "I'm a messenger. My duty is to do what Jesus did. I've got to be about my Father's business."

Mr. T doesn't just talk about his faith. He lives it, too, trying to help poor and sick children especially. "I don't want to be remembered by this world for my toughness or my gold chains, but for how I helped people," he says.

Mr. T puts a lot of effort into keeping himself in shape for this work. He exercises every day. He eats a high-protein diet with lots of fresh fruit, very little sugar, and no alcohol or cigarettes. And he's strongly against drug abuse.

Mr. T hasn't let fame swell his head. He hesitates to give autographs. "I don't feel I'm so great," he once said. "So how can I make you feel great just because you've got my signature on a piece of paper?"

Mr. T's latest movie is *The Toughest Man in the World*. He's working on his autobiography, called *The Bodyguard*.

Behind the Screen: We Interrupt This Book....

Television is a business. Its main purpose is to make money.

Most of television's money comes from advertisers. An advertiser may pay a station or network hundreds of thousands of dollars for the 30 seconds of air time it takes to show their commercial.

The advertiser is paying for time — your time. The advertiser wants you to see the commercial and then go out and buy what's advertised. Some of the money you spend on that advertised product helps pay for more commercials. That's one reason advertised products are often more expensive than unadvertised or "store" brands. (So much for "free" TV.)

Advertising may be the most important thing on TV, but no one wants to sit and watch commercials all day. So stations and networks take some of the advertising money and give it to producers. The producers hire writers, actors, and all of the other people it takes to make a program. They make situation comedies, dramas, action-adventure programs, documentaries, news shows, and all of the other shows that will keep you watching for the next commercial.

The more viewers (possible customers) a station or network has, the more an advertiser is willing to pay for commercials shown on that station or network. Advertisers subscribe to market research companies like Arbitron or the A.C. Nielsen Company to find out how many possible customers are tuned in. Programs with larger audiences are said to have higher *ratings*.

Every "commercial" station and network wants to have the highest ratings so it can make the most money. Stations and networks watch the ratings as carefully as advertisers do. They put on programs that they hope will get the highest ratings. Most shows that are canceled disappear because not enough people watched. "Not enough" could be 20 or 30 million people, but that's still fewer people than are watching another channel.

All viewers are important to television, but some are more important than others. To television, the most important viewers are women between 18 and 49 years old. Statistics show that these viewers spend the most money on advertisers' products, so more television programs are designed to attract these viewers, and more commercials are aimed at them. Sometimes the kind of advertising a show carries is the best clue to which viewers it is trying to attract. Who is the show designed for that has commercials for laundry detergent, beauty products, and supermarket sales? Who is the show for that has commercials for beer and car repairs? What about the show that advertises sugary breakfast cereals and toys?

Much of TV may be connected to advertising, but there's nothing necessarily wrong with that. Both commercials and programs can inform you, entertain you, or educate you. They can bring you to places and show you things you might never otherwise see. Television has been called a "window on the world." That just might be worth paying for.

A Diff'rent Look at Gary Coleman

Arnold Jackson (Gary Coleman), on NBC's *Diff'rent Strokes*, seems to be living the "good" life. He lives in a fancy penthouse apartment on New York's ritzy Park Avenue. He has a loving family and a housekeeper to do the chores. He's even met Mr. T.

But Arnold has paid a high price for this life. He traded almost everything he had for it — parents, home, friends, the works. Of course, he didn't choose to make the trade, but that's still how it happened.

Arnold's father died when Arnold was very young. Arnold and his brother, Willis (Todd Bridges), were brought up by their mother who worked as a housekeeper. Her boss was Phillip Drummond (Conrad Bain), a wealthy businessman who had a young daughter, Kimberly (Dana Plato). When Mrs. Jackson died in 1978, Phillip Drummond brought her sons into his home and adopted them.

Arnold changed schools, friends, family, and lifestyle. He made these changes easily. In fact, if you think about it, he made these huge changes a lot more easily than most people make *little* changes. That's the way things happen on TV.

Six years after the premiere of *Diff'rent Strokes*, Arnold is still going through changes. He's had to accept the fact that he's growing very slowly and will always be pretty small. He's had to deal with problems other kids have, of learning to stand by your friends, and to survive falling in love for the first time. Now Arnold's family has changed again. Phillip Drummond has remarried. Arnold has a new mother, Maggie (Dixie Carter), and a new younger brother, Sam (Danny Cooksey).

Arnold will survive these changes like the other ones. He'll find the fun in them. And we'll have fun watching. That's how it is with TV.

In real life, coping easily with changes takes a lot of

spunk and a sense of humor that never quits. **Gary Coleman**, who plays Arnold Jackson, has both.

Gary has had serious medical problems since he was born. He had a kidney transplant when he was about six years old, and he needed another one last year. The kidney problems have affected his growth. He will not get much taller than five feet. Gary doesn't let this get him down. "What's wrong with being five feet?" he asks.

Gary started modeling when he was five years old. His modeling jobs led to TV commercials, which led to an award and to *Diff'rent Strokes*, which also led to an award. He was named "Best Young Comedian" in 1981.

Gary works hard on his series during the year, and every summer vacation he makes a TV movie. He was *The Kid from Left Field* in 1979. He starred in *Scout's Honor* in 1980, *The Kid with the Broken Halo* in 1981, *The Kid with the 200 I.Q.* in 1982, and *The Fantastic World of D.C. Collins* in 1983. His latest TV movie is *Playing with Fire*. Gary gets to play an older character in this one, which makes him happy. Although he's 16, he plays a 13-year-old on *Diff'rent Strokes*.

Gary's made two feature films, *On the Right Track* and *Jimmy the Kid*. You'd think he's definitely made up his mind to be an actor forever, right? Not necessarily. Gary is also interested in directing, producing, and operating a camera. He already has his own production company, called Zephyr Productions. And, totally aside from show business, he keeps up his model train collection and thinks about going to college to learn a trade.

Gary Coleman hasn't just got spunk and a sense of humor. He's got a lot of energy!

He isn't even 10 years old yet, but **Danny Cooksey** is already into his second career. He's playing Arnold's new brother, Sam, on *Diff'rent Strokes*.

Danny started out as a country-western singer. He's performed with Mickey Gilley; Johnny Lee; Merle Haggard; Hank Williams, Jr.; and Hoyt Axton.

Diff'rent Strokes isn't Danny's first TV show, though it's his first regular role. He's also been on *That's Incredible* and *The Dukes of Hazzard*.

Some Facts About Nancy McKeon

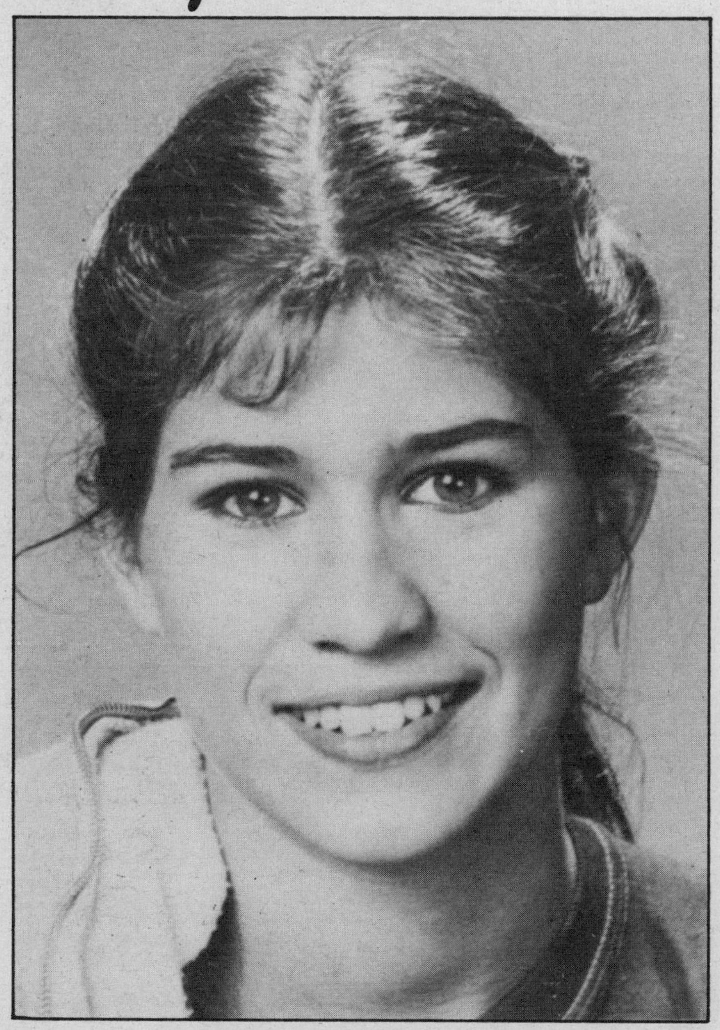

One of the facts of life is that as you get older, you move into new situations. So it's not surprising that a series called *The Facts of Life* (NBC) has done the same thing.

It's been six years since Edna Garrett (Charlotte Rae) left her job as housekeeper for Phillip Drummond. (Yes, that's the same Phillip Drummond from *Diff'rent Strokes. The Facts of Life* is a spinoff of that series.) She went on to work as a housemother at the exclusive — and fictional — Eastland School for Girls in New York.

The next year, Mrs. Garrett became school dietitian. She was still the adult-in-charge of four of the school's students — Blair (Lisa Whelchel), Jo (Nancy McKeon), Natalie (Mindy Cohn), and Tootie (Kim Fields). Mrs. Garrett put the girls to work for her in the dining room. In return, she helped solve their problems with dating, money, honesty, and friendship.

Last year, Blair and Jo graduated from Eastland and went on to a nearby college. Mrs. Garrett left her job at Eastland and opened a gourmet shop, Edna's Edibles. It looked like the Eastland Five was splitting up for good.

The split-up didn't last long. The whole idea behind a "situation comedy" is that the *comedy* comes from the *situation* that every character shares. It just so

happened that Edna's Edibles had a big upstairs. Big enough for Mrs. Garrett to live in. Big enough for her to have four boarders — Blair, Jo, Natalie, and Tootie.

Now the girls work for Mrs. Garrett in her shop. They're learning a lot about running a business — especially Jo. They still don't go to many classes or seem to have much homework, though. Oh, well. How many facts of life can you fit into half an hour a week, after all?

It was good business for **Nancy McKeon** to take the role of Jo on *The Facts of Life*. She's become one of the most popular teens on TV. Her portrayal of a determined student and worker, with brains but not much money, really appeals to viewers.

Now 18, Nancy started working as a model when she was two years old. Her older brother, Philip, got work on a TV series before she did, though. He got the part of Tommy on the series *Alice*. It meant that the family had to move from Long Island to California. "I was happy for Philip," Nancy says, "but it meant I had to start all over again. For a long time, nothing happened. I thought of quitting."

Philip urged Nancy to stay in show business. In 1979 she got her role on *The Facts of Life*, and she's been working steadily ever since. In her time off from the series, she's made afterschool and nighttime TV specials, like *Schoolboy Father* and *Please Don't Hit Me, Mom*. And she's done voices for cartoon characters on ABC Weekend Specials.

Nancy would like to work in feature films. And she'd like to do more work with her brother. (She guest-starred once in an episode of *Alice*.) One way or another, show business is a fact of Nancy's life. She has a simple way to explain that: "I love it."

20

Behind the Screen: Who's Watching What?

"We got a phone call from someone at the A.C. Nielsen Company," Janet Galen said. "She told us a viewing diary was in the mail to us and asked us to please read the instructions and fill out the diary for a week. We said we didn't watch much television, but she asked us to do it anyway."

The next day, Janet and her husband got a package from Nielsen. "There was a letter thanking us for participating," Janet said. "There was a small staple-bound diary and an envelope with postage paid to return the diary in. There was also a little 'thank-you' present — 50 cents."

The diary covered seven days. Each day was divided into 15-minute sections. "There was a place on the page for each person who lives in the house to write in what they watched," Janet said. "We were supposed to fill in the whole day. If the TV was off, we were supposed to say so.

"They wanted to know what program we watched, which 15-minute segments of the program we watched, the number of the channel we were watching, and the station's call letters. They also wanted to know how many TVs we have, and what rooms they're in. At the end of the week, there was space for comments about how we felt about TV in general — anything we wanted to say."

Janet and her husband were chosen at random to be a Nielsen family last February. During most of the year, Nielsen surveys 2,600 families at a time with diaries. (Another 1,700 families have Audimeters attached to their TV sets. The Audimeters are connected to a central computer and tell when the TV is on or off, and which channel it's turned to.) February is a special "sweeps" period, as are May, July, and November. Sweeps are super-surveys that give a closer look at Americans' viewing habits. During sweeps periods, 220,000 families are asked to fill out diaries. The information obtained during sweeps periods provides data about what people are watching on local stations across the country.

"Being a Nielsen family was fun," Janet said. "It made us more aware of what was on TV and what we wanted to watch."

You can't ask to be a Nielsen family, but you can learn more about how Nielsen works by writing to:

Press Relations
The A.C. Nielsen Company
1290 Avenue of the Americas
New York, New York 10104

Stations, networks, and advertisers use the Nielsen ratings in general — and sweeps results in particular — to decide which programs to keep or cancel. Ratings also help determine how much money advertisers should be charged to show their commercials. The stations and networks with the highest ratings can charge more.

One specific thing sweeps also do is tell what programs young people like to watch. Most-watched programs during the most recent February sweeps were:

Among ages 6–11	*How many watched (rating)*
# 1 — Is This Good-bye, Charlie Brown?	33.7%
# 2 — Disney's Valentine Party	31.8%
# 3 — How Bugs Bunny Won the West	31.6%
# 4 — Berenstain Bears Valentine Special	27.9%
# 5 — The A-Team	27.8%
# 6 — Knight Rider	27.5%
# 7 — Bugs Bunny/Road Runner Movie	25.7%
# 8 — The Making of Superman III	23.7%
# 9 — Silver Spoons	23.4%
#10 — Diff'rent Strokes	22.6%
#10 — ABC Movie Specials	22.6%
#11 — The Dukes of Hazzard	21.3%
#12 — Webster	20.6%
#13 — Bugs Bunny Valentine	20.4%
#14 — Be My Valentine, Charlie Brown	20.0%
#15 — NBC Friday Night Movie	19.2%
#16 — Charlie Brown Celebration	18.9%
#17 — Benson	18.8%
#17 — I Love Chipmunks Valentine	18.8%
#18 — Three's Company	17.3%

Among ages 12–17	*How many watched (rating)*
# 1 — American Music Awards	35.1%
# 2 — ABC Movie Specials	27.0%
# 3 — The A-Team	22.6%
# 4 — Silver Spoons	21.2%
# 5 — New Year's Rockin' Eve '84	21.0%
# 6 — Life's Most Embarrassing Moments	20.2%
# 7 — Diff'rent Strokes	19.9%
# 8 — Knight Rider	19.7%
# 9 — The Facts of Life	18.5%
# 9 — Three's Company	18.5%
#10 — TV Bloopers and Practical Jokes	18.4%
#11 — Winter Olympics	17.5%
#12 — Webster	17.4%
#13 — Is This Good-bye, Charlie Brown?	17.1%
#14 — The Fall Guy	16.6%
#14 — CBS Special Movie Presentation	16.6%
#15 — NBC Friday Night Movie	16.5%
#16 — How Bugs Bunny Won the West	16.4%
#17 — Riptide	16.3%
#18 — Happy Days	15.1%

Source: A.C. Nielsen Co. National Audience Demographics Report, February 1984.

Nell Carter Gets a Break

There have been two extra-special food-related commercials on TV this year. In one, a woman we could see demanded, "Where's the beef?" This ad sold a lot of hamburgers. In the other, a woman we couldn't see invited us to "Slip into something irresistible," and try a diet soft drink. The star of the first commercial was Clara Peller, who suddenly became a celebrity. The slinky-voiced star of the other commercial was already well-known. She's **Nell Carter**, star of *Gimme a Break* (NBC).

Nell started out as a singer. She moved to New York from her home in Birmingham, Alabama, and worked in musical theater. She won a Tony Award in the show

Ain't Misbehavin', and later starred in the TV production of that show.

Nell left singing behind for a while when she took a role in the TV series *Lobo*, a spin-off of *BJ and the Bear*. Three years ago, she got her own series, *Gimme a Break*.

Gimme a Break has gone through some changes since the first season. Nell's character, called Nell Harper, was a not-too-efficient housekeeper with a loving heart. She'd been hired by a recently widowed police chief (Dolph Sweet) to care for his three daughters (Kari Michaelsen, Lauri Hendler, and Lara Jill Miller). Several of the early episodes dealt with loss in general and death in particular in a very sensitive way.

Since then, the show has concentrated more on being funny. Nell's character has become less of a substitute mother. She has other things to do besides care for the girls and Joey (Joey Lawrence), a young runaway brought into the family last season. Nell Harper has taken off weight, fallen in love, and done some singing on the show. A flashback episode showed that she was friends with the chief's wife when the girls were younger. The chief's wife knew she was dying and asked Nell to help raise her children afterwards. Nell wasn't sure she wanted to do it. She was hoping for a singing career. But she doesn't seem to regret her choice now. And with all her singing in recent episodes, it looks as if she might have that career after all.

One reason *Gimme a Break* changed was that the audience wanted it to. "Why do black women only get to play maids?" people protested. "Black women can do many other things. Nell has many talents. Let's see some of them!" The producers seemed to agree.

Nell still sings "Gimme a Break!" in the show's theme song, but now she's playing a character who has a chance to stretch herself and try new things.

The Big Little Star of Webster

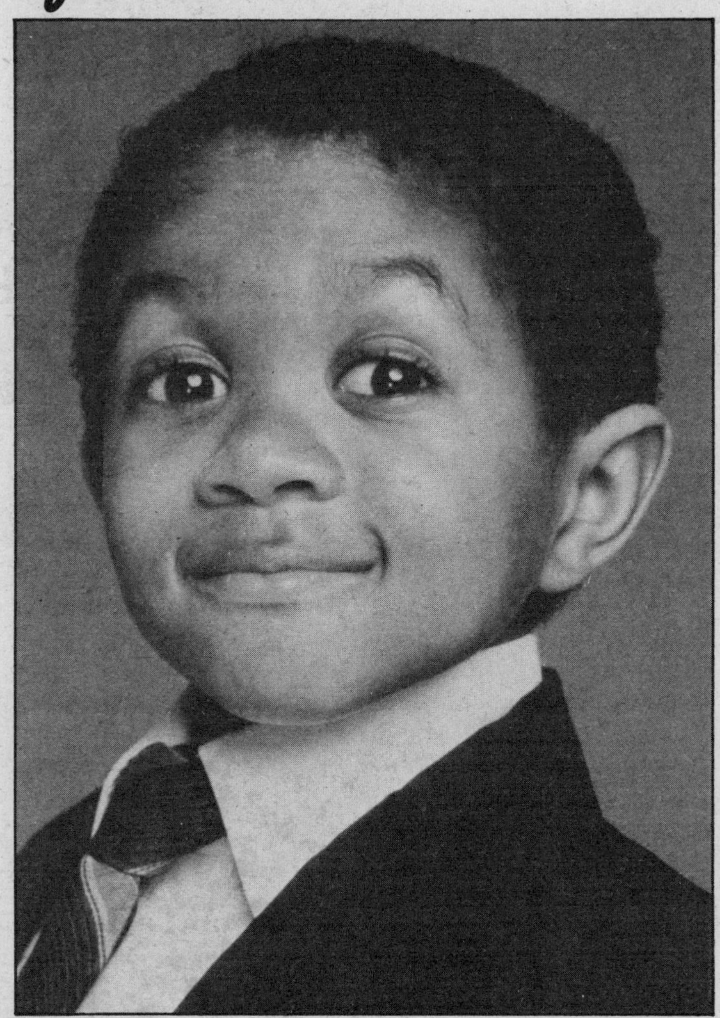

Webster (ABC) is *not* a clone of *Diff'rent Strokes*. Okay, both shows have small, cute, smart-talking kids in starring roles. They're both orphans, they're both black, and they've both been adopted by rich, white New York families. They're both going through the problems of changing their lives and growing up. But they're very different, too!

Webster may be the only situation comedy that tries to deal realistically with the problems of becoming an instant family. It's often been very hard to tell how Katherine Calder-Young Papadapolis (Susan Clark) — Ma'am — really feels about her new son. After all, she had just met and married George (Alex Karras, Susan Clark's real-life husband) when Webster came to live with them. She had a busy career that she didn't want to give up. She'd never planned to be a mother. The recent battle over Webster's custody with his Uncle Philip (Ben Vereen) helped Katherine figure out how she really feels. Now she's growing to love and understand Webster. Meanwhile, the program is showing how hard these problems can be to resolve.

Emmanuel Lewis' biggest problem could be growing too fast. It happened to his brother when *he* was 13. (That's Emmanuel's age now.) Emmanuel's brother grew seven inches in one year. Being able to watch yourself grow could be interesting. It could also be painful. And it could mean rewriting some of the main ideas in your TV series.

Emmanuel was 12 when he started playing Webster last year. Webster was seven. There were other differences between them besides age. "He's much more formal than I am," Emmanuel says. "I'm funnier — I hope."

Emmanuel became a professional actor in 1980. An actor friend sent him to an agent. The agent sent Emmanuel to try out for a commercial. The producers hired him right away, and he's been working ever since. This year you could see his burger commercials all over the dial.

Emmanuel is also a singer and a dancer. He is a popular recording star — in Japan. He's had three hit records there. He's also made commercials and a movie for Japanese TV.

Emmanuel seems to be comfortable anywhere. He's acted on stage in Shakespeare's *A Midsummer Night's Dream* and he's been interviewed on *The Tonight Show* and the *Donahue* show.

So getting suddenly taller might not be a problem for Emmanuel after all. His talent is big already.

Behind the Screen: Star Chemistry

What makes a TV series successful? Exciting stories? Gorgeous actors? Fancy settings? All of these things help. But it's hard to have a successful TV series unless there's also good chemistry between the actors in the main roles.

"Chemistry" is that hard-to-define something that makes characters seem to fit together just right. When that magical thing happens, you almost don't care what the characters *do*. You just like seeing them together.

Tom Selleck and John Hillerman have good chemistry on *Magnum, P.I.* So do Robert Guillaume and Inga Swenson on *Benson*. Henry Winkler and Ron Howard had such good chemistry on *Happy Days* that the producers were afraid to split them up. They had an idea for a spin-off show for the character of the Fonz, but decided against it because they thought he might not make it without Richie. However, *Happy Days* turned out to be successful for years after Ron Howard left. He didn't take *all* of the chemistry with him. There were still Fonzie and Chachi, Chachi and Joanie, Marion and Howard....

You don't have to be human to have a good chemical reaction. The best thing going for *Knight Rider* is the

chemistry between David Hasselhoff and a Pontiac Trans Am. And one of the nicest parts of *Riptide* is the chemistry between Thom Bray and the robot Roboz.

When the actors have good chemistry, it almost doesn't matter if the story idea is silly. It almost doesn't matter if the plot doesn't make sense. You may still enjoy the show. But if the characters don't have good chemistry, it almost doesn't matter how good everything else is. The production is going to be boring.

So it's simple, right? Just find actors with good chemistry.

It's not so simple after all. Chemistry isn't something one actor has alone. (That's called "charisma.") It's something that happens between actors. Actor A can have terrific chemistry with Actor B and seem dull with Actor C. Mariette Hartley and James Garner had wonderful chemistry in those camera commercials, for instance. But when Mariette teamed up with Bill Bixby in *Goodnight, Beantown* last season, sparks didn't fly. Neither did the show.

Actors with good chemistry create something new and fresh — a good TV show. That's the kind you'll probably choose to watch whenever you have the chance.

Investigating Scarecrow and Mrs. King

Amanda King (Kate Jackson) met government agent Lee Stetson — code name Scarecrow (Bruce Boxleitner) — at the train station. She was in a hurry because she was wearing pajamas under her raincoat. She wanted to get home and go back to sleep. Scarecrow was in a hurry because he was being chased by enemy agents. They wanted to kill him, or at least get possession of the box he was carrying.

Amanda and Scarecrow had an unusual introduction. He shoved the box into her hands, told her to give it to the man in the red hat already on the train, and disappeared. Amanda didn't realize it, but this was her first step in getting a new job. It's called "being-in-the-right-place-at-the-right-time."

Since then, the government agent and the housewife/mother-of-two have saved the fate of the free world many times. They make a good team. He has years of training and experience. She has good instincts and a lot of luck. Between them, they have a nice chemistry. It makes *Scarecrow and Mrs. King* (CBS) a spy series with a sense of humor that's fun to watch.

When **Kate Jackson** was one of *Charlie's Angels*, she was known as "the smart one." As Amanda King, she uses luck and instinct to solve her cases. All of these qualities have helped Kate in her own career.

She grew up in Birmingham, Alabama, and always knew she wanted to act. The two best places to find acting work are New York and Los Angeles, so at the end of her teens, Kate moved to New York.

She studied acting at the American Academy of Dramatic Arts and soon got a part on the soap opera *Dark Shadows*. "I was a terrific ghost for nine months," she says. Then she moved to Los Angeles.

Kate's first regular series was on *The Rookies*. That led to her part as Sabrina Duncan on *Charlie's Angels*. Kate left the show in 1979 to work on her own projects.

The first was a TV movie called *Topper*, based on an earlier movie and TV series. Kate starred with her then-husband, Andrew Stevens. They played a couple of terrific ghosts.

In addition to *Topper*, Kate made the TV movies *Killer Bees*, *The New Healers*, *James at 15*, *Thin Ice*, and *Listen to Your Heart*. She was keeping busy and doing well but wanted to work even harder, so she accepted the role of Amanda on *Scarecrow and Mrs. King*. She got her wish to work hard. It's not unusual for Kate to work 12 or 14 hours a day, even on weekends.

That doesn't leave her with much time to furnish her new house or help run her Shoot the Moon production company. But Kate enjoys her job. She loves the series and the fact that some episodes were filmed in Europe last summer.

Kate Jackson has made a success of her career. Amanda King would understand Kate's explanation: "Be in the right place at the right time, and be ready."

Bruce Boxleitner has been the good guy in both of his latest TV series, *Bring 'Em Back Alive* and *Scarecrow and Mrs. King*. He enjoys playing a hero. One of his own heroes is the ultimate good guy, John Wayne.

Bruce's first role on TV was a guest part on *The Mary Tyler Moore Show*. He's also guest-starred on shows like *Police Woman* and *Hawaii Five-O*. On those programs, he usually played the victim or the bad guy.

Bruce had a role in the mini-series *How the West Was Won*. It led to his playing the same character, Luke Macahan, for two years on the series *The Macahans*. It also led to his marriage to Kathryn Holcomb, who played his sister on the series.

Between TV series, Bruce made other TV movies and mini-series, like *Bare Essence* (with Genie Francis), *East of Eden*, and *Kenny Rogers as the Gambler, Parts 1 and 2*. He also starred in the feature film *Tron*.

Behind the Screen: TV's Mechanical Stars

And now, the nominees for best performance in an action-adventure series. The finalists are General Lee, KITT, RALF, Airwolf, Blue Thunder, and Screaming Mimi.

The contestants in this category should be judged on the basis of speed, intelligence, ability to defend themselves, and, of course, miles per gallon.

A "hardware show" sounds like a place you go to look at wrenches. These days, though, it's something else. It's one of the most popular kinds of television programming.

Who would have thought that cars, computers, motorcycles, and helicopters could become some of our favorite TV stars? Airwolf and Blue Thunder even had their own shows named for them. What's going on here? We know that machines are taking over some jobs. Are they getting ready to replace actors?

Probably not. Last time we checked, people still liked watching *people*. But machines do make good co-stars.

First of all, they're fun to look at. Their outsides are interesting, especially when they're painted like the *Dukes of Hazzard*'s General Lee or *Riptide*'s Screaming Mimi.

Next, it's fun to try to figure out how they work. Could you have programmed *Whiz Kids'* RALF? Could you fly Airwolf? (To be fair, nobody could. The technology doesn't exist — at least, not yet....)

Machines also add excitement to a show. Watching *Knight Rider's* KITT in a chase scene can be like taking a roller coaster ride in your living room. Could you get as involved if Michael chased — or was chased by — the bad guys on foot?

The importance of machines on TV reflects the importance of machines in our lives. It makes sense to see TV characters who depend on their cars or their computers. Doesn't everyone have some kind of machine that's important in their life — even if it's "only" a telephone, refrigerator, elevator — or television set!

The machine stars on TV are always good guys. That's important, too. For instance, computers are so new that many people still don't understand them. Computers make them nervous. But how could Roboz or KITT make you nervous? Maybe some people like watching hardware shows because the shows help them feel better about the hardware in their lives.

Whatever the reasons, one thing is clear: Hardware shows are popular. *And so, the envelope, please.*

The Knight Riders

One of the best episodes of *Knight Rider* (NBC) was the one in which Michael (David Hasselhoff) had amnesia. He forgot that he used to be a cop but wasn't anymore. He forgot that he was so badly hurt in his last police assignment that he had had plastic surgery that changed his face. He forgot that he now worked as a law enforcement agent for Knight Industries. He forgot that his new partner was the Knight Industries Two Thousand — KITT — a computerized Pontiac Trans Am with intelligence, the ability to speak, and a heart.

The best part of the episode was when KITT gently helped Michael to regain his memory. KITT used humor, affection, and loyalty to do the job. Too bad KITT's just a car. He seems like the best friend anyone could have.

In fact, Michael and KITT make one of the best teams on television. Their chemistry is excellent. It also may be surprising. The actors who play the roles do their parts separately!

Michael is played by **David Hasselhoff**. David was Snapper Foster on the soap opera *The Young and the Restless* for six years. *Knight Rider* is his second prime-time (evening) series. He was also in *Semi-Tough*, a four-episode show based on the movie of the same name.

When David's not working on *Knight Rider*, he may be spending time with his new bride, actress Catherine Hickland (Julie Clegg McCandless on *Capitol*). She's been a guest-star on *Knight Rider*, too. David's also working on a singing career. He performed "No Way To Be in Love," a song he wrote, on an episode last spring.

David visits with children in the hospital. And he helps run a company that sells a kind of baseball that won't hurt when it hits you.

All around, he's doing good work.

The bad news is that there's no such real car as KITT — at least, not so far. The good news is that KITT's voice belongs to a real actor, one you can see on another show. He's **William Daniels**, and he plays Dr. Mark Craig on *St. Elsewhere* (NBC). Daniels started acting when he was four years old. He's been on the stage, in movies, and on television. There's a good chance you've seen him as John Adams in the movie *1776*. It's shown every year on television.

When he isn't working, Daniels spends time with his wife, actress Bonnie Bartlett. Actually, they often spend time together when they *are* working, too. She plays Ellen Craig, Mark Craig's wife, on *St. Elsewhere*.

How Debbie Allen Found Fame

Debbie Allen's character is different from any other character on TV. She has a special kind of comfortableness in the way she talks, dresses, and moves. She has a special reason for this, too.

Debbie plays Lydia Grant on *Fame*. Lydia is a teacher in the program's School of the Arts. Like Debbie, she's a dancer.

Dancers often seem more comfortable with themselves than other people do. But something extra is happening here. Even though *Fame* has a large cast, Lydia is one of the most important characters in every episode.

Fame is about the work it takes to put on the performance that ends each episode. There are other story lines — Bruno's father dying, or Danny fighting cancer — but every story leads to a production number at the end (with plenty of rehearsals along the way).

A production number has lots of singing, dancing, and costumes. Putting the moves together and mak-

ing sure they come out right — choreography — is Lydia's job. It's also Debbie's, since Debbie is the choreographer for *Fame*.

Debbie's role wasn't always so large. She was in the cast of the movie *Fame*, on which the series is based. She had a one-word part. She played the part so well that she was asked to be in the series. Debbie said she would do it if she could choreograph, too.

Debbie knew she had the ability. She really has been a dance instructor at a school for talented kids. All she needed now was the chance.

As Lydia, Debbie does what she knows best. *And* she is in charge of the part of *Fame* that makes it special. These things give Debbie/Lydia a reason for an extra look of confidence. That confidence keeps Lydia interesting to watch, no matter what else is going on in the episode.

Confidence isn't something Debbie Allen found on *Fame* — though maybe the show has helped her to increase it. Confidence is what helped her get the job. And it shows.

Behind the Screen:
Music Television

Fame was doing something unusual when it included music and dancing in its first episode, in January 1981. Now prime-time shows and soap operas all over the dial are getting into the act. And if just a little music with your television isn't enough, you can also turn to television for *only* music. There are suddenly over 200 music-video programs shown on channels around the country. Most of them were started because of the success of MTV.

MTV (Music Television) is a 24-hour-a-day basic cable channel that specializes in video rock. It started in August 1981, looking something like a radio station with pictures. Instead of disc jockeys, MTV uses video jockeys to talk about music and artists and to introduce songs. Instead of just playing records by your favorite rock groups, MTV plays video versions of the songs.

MTV (and other rock video programs) get their rock videos free from record companies. Videos help promote the sale of records. (That's why these free copies are called "promotion copies." Radio stations get promotion copies of records for the same reason.) Seeing the performers and hearing the songs makes people want their own copies.

Videos may be free to rock-video programs, but they can cost from $10,000 to $1,500,000 to make. Because they're expensive and have a big job to do, rock videos have to look good — or at least exciting. Making the video good enough, or exciting enough, to help promote record sales has become an important part of being a rock musician. Some songwriters have started working with video directors before a song is even finished, to make sure all the pieces will fit together in the end.

Still, the images in many rock videos have very little to do with the words of the song. A lot of videos use horror stories or violence in the effort to be memorable. Then you might have to ask what the video has to do with the song. The answer is often, "Not much."

Some artists who are using videos to help illustrate their songs are also helping to create a whole new kind of television. Their videos use new camera techniques and computer graphics. Videos like Michael Jackson's "Thriller," Rick Springfield's "Souls," and Paul Simon's "René and Georgette Magritte with Their Dog After the War" would be fun to watch even without the songs (though not as much).

Videos don't just sell records. Rock fans with video-cassette recorders want to buy the videos themselves. Now they can. Sony was the first company to come out with a video 45, a cassette with three to five songs and up to 20 minutes of video music.

Rock music is no longer just for listening.

The Dreams of John Stamos

"I'd like to be a successful musician," **John Stamos** has said. He could have been speaking for himself; for his last character, Blackie Parrish on *General Hospital*; or for his latest character, Gino Minelli. The *Dreams* (CBS) of all three seem to be coming together in John's new series. Gino is the leader of a Philadelphia rock 'n' roll band that's starting to make it. The show is interesting both for the way it fits in with John's real dreams, and for the way it looks. *Dreams* is the first TV series to use techniques invented by MTV and rock videos.

John started his life in show business behind the scenes. At the age of five, he became a puppeteer. He was so good at it that he was soon performing professionally. At 10, he came out in front of the curtain to practice magic, which he also performed professionally.

Meanwhile, John was learning to play the drums. He helped form his first rock band, Destiny, when he was in junior high school. A few years later, he expanded his activities into acting, performing in high school plays.

It was a visit to the set of *Happy Days* that made John decide to become an actor when school was finished. He took acting lessons, found an agent, and began working in commercials.

The role of Blackie on *GH* started out as a short assignment. John was supposed to work for only five days. But the audience fell in love with Blackie, even though, John says, he started out as a "real bad, hard-nosed kind of guy." John wound up playing him for two years. Along the way, Blackie "straightened out a little, but he still [kept his] tough streak." John got an Emmy nomination for his portrayal of Blackie in 1983. He won the 1983 Soapy Award for most exciting newcomer.

Behind the Screen: TV's New Technology

Being a serious television watcher used to be easy. You had a choice between black-and-white or color, and a handful of programs. It's different now. By the time you figure out all the new services, special features, and extra channels, your favorite program could be over. Don't panic. Here's a mini-guide to television's new technology.

Broadcast TV: What you get when you turn on your ordinary TV set. The signal comes through the air to your TV's antenna from local stations or channels. When local stations from different areas join together and broadcast the same programs, they're called **networks**. The three major networks are ABC, CBS, and NBC. Stations that are part of a network are called network **affiliates**. Stations that are not part of a network are called **independents**.

Cable: Basic cable is a system that sends a television signal into your TV set over a wire, like the telephone, instead of over the air, like broadcast TV. When cable TV started, in the 1940s, it was called **CATV** (community antenna television). It was invented to improve TV reception in places where broadcast signals couldn't reach (for example, where hills or mountains got in the way). Today cable TV offers improved reception and extra channels to people who choose it (subscribers) and pay about $6 to $10 a month. Cable makes it possible to add other services and programs for additional fees. In order to get cable TV, your community must be specially wired. Then you may subscribe through a local cable operator, called a **franchiser**.

Closed-captioning: The subtitling of certain TV shows so deaf or hearing-impaired viewers may enjoy them. The subtitles don't distract hearing viewers because you need special decoders to make them appear on your screen.

DBS: Direct broadcast satellites. TV signals are beamed up to a satellite in orbit around the earth. The satellite turns the signal around and sends it into the small **receiving dishes**, or **earth stations**, that subscribers have set up on their roofs or in their yards. Because the satellite is up so high, it can send its signal into the many homes beneath it in its **footprint**, or receiving area. The part of the satellite that sends the signal back to earth is the **transponder**. Most satellites have 24 transponders. Each one can transmit one TV channel. DBS allows national programming without having to use local stations or cable systems.

HDTV: High definition TV. Regular American TV pictures are actually made up of 525 lines of dots. High definition TV is an improvement to TV sets that gives up to 1,125 lines of dots. It makes the TV picture much sharper and clearer.

Interactive television: Services like two-way cable (QUBE, electronic shopping, teleconferencing), videotex (see below), or videodiscs (see below) that let you talk to people directly through your TV.

LPTV: Low power TV. Stations that send a weak signal and reach only a small area. They don't interfere with channels already there, but do make it possible to bring extra programming to the area.

MDS: Multipoint distribution service. A signal sent by microwaves, which can travel about 25 miles from the sending point. MDS is not very expensive, but tall buildings, trees, and hills can interfere with reception.

MSO: Multiple system operator. A cable company that owns several systems in several communities, not just one.

Narrowcasting: Channels that carry programs aimed at only one part of the audience are *narrow*casting rather than *broad*casting. MTV (Music Television) is a 24-hour channel just for rock fans. Nickelodeon is a channel just for kids. Broadcast stations carry shows for different parts of the audience at different times of the day.

Pay cable: Special cable channels for which you pay an extra fee beyond the basic cable fee. MTV and public access channels (see below) are part of basic cable. HBO (Home Box Office) and Showtime/The Movie Channel are pay cable services. You must have basic cable to get pay cable, but you don't have to get pay cable if you have basic. Pay cable channels are usually offered in groups called **tiers** (steps), because you add them on top of basic cable services.

Pay-per-view: A service made simple by interactive cable, though it's also possible on one-way cable channels and through STV (see below). The channel operator sends out programs in scrambled form. Unless you have an unscrambler, all you see is static. You arrange to have the programs you want to see unscrambled for you. You pay only for unscrambled shows.

Pay television: Programs for which subscribers pay a fee — cable, SMATV (see below), MDS, STV, or DBS. (Broadcast TV is called "free" TV, but it isn't really free when you take into consideration the extra money you pay for advertised products.)

Public access: Channels that anyone (like *you*!) can use for a slight fee. Public access channels are part of every basic cable service. You apply to the cable company, and they schedule a time for you. The company usually lets you use its equipment and people, and those people will help you with the technical questions. But *you* decide what your program is about.

SMATV: Satellite master-antenna TV. "Private cable" to apartments. TV programs are sent to the apartment building by satellite. Cable wires attached to the antenna on the roof bring the programs into individual apartments.

STV: Subscription TV. A pay television service that doesn't require cable. Subscribers get decoding boxes that unscramble programs on otherwise unused channels on their TV sets.

Superstation: A local broadcast station that uses cable and satellite to reach viewers all over the country. WTBS in Atlanta sends its signal up to a satellite as well as over the air. Cable companies around the country take the WTBS satellite signal and pass it along to their subscribers.

Teletext: News, weather, sports, videogames, stock market prices, and other information sent on the black band you see when the horizontal hold on your TV set needs adjusting. You need a decoder to receive this service. **Videotex** (also called **viewdata**) is a kind of expanded, two-way teletext. It uses telephone lines to connect your TV to a central computer. Videotex makes it possible to do banking, shopping, research, and other interactive transactions at home.

UHF: Ultra-high frequency. TV channels 14–69.

VHF: Very-high frequency. TV channels 2–13.

VCR: Video cassette recorder. A machine that attaches to your TV set so you can record programs, or play pre-recorded programs. VCRs make it possible to **time-shift** — watch a program when it's convenient for you, not when a station decides to schedule it. There are two basic kinds of VCR machines — **Beta** and **VHS** (video home system). The tapes from one won't run on the other.

Videodisc: An interactive video record. You don't have to watch it straight through, but can choose which part to see, and in which order.

Michael J. Fox and Justine Bateman Have Strong Family Ties

No matter how great your folks are, or how much you love them, sooner or later there's a time when you feel as if you have to be *yourself*, somebody separate and different from them. This usually happens when you're a teenager.

It happened to Elyse Donnelly (Meredith Baxter Birney) and Steven Keaton (Michael Gross). They grew up in the 1960s. They saw the proper, buttoned-down look of their parents and their parents' friends. They thought the ideas the older generation had were just as proper and buttoned-down. Steven and Elyse didn't think that was good. They wanted to be their own persons, do their own things.

Steven and Elyse started wearing casual clothes. They let their hair grow. They tried to be less "uptight." They wanted to "go with the flow."

They were still responsible people, though. Elyse became an architect. Steven went to work in public television. They got married and had three children. They expected their kids to be happy with the kind of world they preferred.

They almost forgot how it was when they were growing up. They forgot that it's normal for kids to question their parents' life-style or the things they believe in.

Alex (Michael J. Fox), Mallory (Justine Bateman), and Jennifer (Tina Yothers) are Elyse and Steven's kids. They're growing up in the 1980s. They're not so sure "buttoned-down" is so bad — especially Alex, the oldest.

It takes a lot of work and a lot of love to keep these people happy together. It takes strong *Family Ties* (NBC). Luckily, that's exactly what they have.

It's not unusual for an actor to have a fan club. But how often do you hear of his *character* having one? What does **Michael J. Fox** think of an Alex P. Keaton fan club? It makes sense to him. People like Alex's conservative but know-it-all attitude, Michael explains.

So does Michael. "He's been the greatest thing that ever happened to me in my career," Michael says.

A few other good things have happened as well. Michael got his first TV role eight years ago. "My drama teacher told me they were looking for a bright 10-year-old," he says. "Being 15, I was definitely the brightest 10-year-old they came across." He got the part, in a Canadian television series called *Leo and Me*.

Michael made a couple of TV movies back home in Vancouver, Canada, too. When he was 18, he moved to Los Angeles. Striking out on his own was easier for him than it would be for some kids. "My father was a sergeant in the army," he says. "We traveled around

the country a lot. I was used to the feeling of being in a new place."

Michael guest-starred in American TV series like *Teachers Only*; *Trapper John, M.D.*; and *Family*. He won the role of Willie-Joe Hall in *Palmerstown, U.S.A.* He made the movies *Midnight Madness* and *The Class of 1984*.

For the moment, Michael is just concentrating on Alex. "I'm doing something I like," he says. He's not in a hurry to move on.

Justine Bateman has done a lot of traveling, too. Her mother is an airline flight attendant, and the love of going places must have rubbed off. Eighteen-year-old Justine has been to Chile, Malta, England, Italy, and Japan.

She hasn't moved around quite so much in her acting career, though. Aside from two TV commercials, Mallory Keaton is her first role. But Justine prepared for a long time. She started studying drama when she was 11. She began working as a model when she was 15.

Unlike Mallory, a reluctant student, Justine enjoys school. She'd like to study photography, psychology, journalism, and drama in college. Still, she has sympathy for Mallory. "It's not that she's an airhead," Justine says. "She just doesn't apply herself. She's a little on the frivolous side. But she's nice."

Justine's brother is Jason Bateman. He's played James Cooper on *Little House on the Prairie* and Derek Taylor on *Silver Spoons*. This fall he stars in his own series, *It's Your Move* (NBC).

All of a Sudden, Three's A Crowd

"**John [Ritter]** was always playing a part," his mother says. "When he'd play baseball, he'd pretend he was one of the Dodgers. By the time he was 12, he and some other kids had already made their first movie."

Actress Dorothy Fay and actor/country-western singer Tex Ritter weren't surprised when their little boy John grew up to be an actor. *He* was, though. John expected to be a psychologist, or maybe a politician.

"I wanted to be President of the United States," John says. He did get as far as being elected student-body president of Hollywood High School. By the time he got to college, though, he'd changed his mind. "I realized I couldn't take myself so seriously."

John majored in drama in college. Between semesters, he worked as an actor in Europe. When school was finished, John performed in plays, movies, and TV series in the United States. He got especially good at playing ministers. John had the recurring role of Reverend Fordwick on *The Waltons*. He played the minister who married Georgette and Ted Baxter on *The Mary Tyler Moore Show*. And he starred as the minister Tom McPherson in the TV movie *Pray TV*.

In the middle of all that, John got the role of Jack Tripper on *Three's Company*. "I give the show about two years," John said when it started. Seven-and-a-half years later, *Three's Company* is still one of the hottest shows in reruns. It's also turned into its own spin-off. John is the only member of the original cast to remain in the retitled and revamped *Three's a Crowd* (ABC).

Three's Company is based on an English series called *Man About the House*. Both shows are about three young people, a man and two women, who live together as friends and help each other into and out of crazy situations.

64

After seven years of being "just friends," Jack Tripper has decided he wants to be married. He didn't fall in love with one of his roommates. Instead, he literally fell in love with airline flight attendant Vicky Bradford (Mary Cadorette) when he stumbled into her arms on a bumpy trip. Now they're "sharing space" until she's ready to set the date for the wedding. The "crowd" part comes in the form of Vicky's father (Robert Mandan). He's the landlord. He doesn't think Jack is good enough for his daughter.

Be that as it may, Jack/John's certainly good enough for us. So we'll keep watching to see how it all turns out.

Behind the Screen: Soaps

Soap operas have been around longer than television has. They may have gotten their first inspiration from the old movie serials. The movie serials had many episodes. They specialized in "cliffhanger" endings, in which a person might literally be left hanging from a cliff when the episode was over! The audience was always eager to see how things would turn out in the next installment.

Then came the daytime dramas on radio. They had many characters and different story lines going on at the same time. The radio dramas had cliffhanger endings every day.

The main audience for these programs was housewives, who would listen to the shows while they worked at home. The programs were called *soaps* because they were sponsored by soap and detergent companies. They were called *operas* because of their dramatic story lines.

Soaps did well on television, too, selling lots of laundry detergent and toothpaste. But in the 1970s more and more women started having careers outside the home. Most people can't watch TV on their jobs; and with fewer housewives at home to tune in, the soap operas had to find a way to build up their audiences.

Today, the most successful soap operas have story lines that feature young actors. They attract a young but large audience — the after-school crowd. They still carry commercials for the household and beauty products for which women do most of the shopping. But they've also added commercials for products that kids buy, like soft drinks and chewing gum.

Young viewers have helped make stars out of soap opera actors. Rick Springfield and John Stamos are recent examples. They became big hits on ABC's *General Hospital*. Then they used their popularity to help them in careers in the movies, the music business, and on prime-time TV.

In 1978, producers and networks started working on a new idea about soaps. If the shows were so popular during the day, they wondered, would similar shows be popular at night, when everyone was home to watch? They decided to put on very dramatic programs with stories that continued into the next weeks, instead of ending after one hour. It was a new idea for nighttime TV, but it looked like it just might work.

The first nighttime soap was *Dallas,* on CBS. It became one of the most popular TV shows in history. Today, the first nighttime soap has been joined by others, like *Knots Landing,* *Falcon Crest,* and *Dynasty.* Even shows like *Hill Street Blues* and *St. Elsewhere* have elements of soap operas. Some of their story lines are longer than one episode. They bring you back the next week, eager to find out what happens next. It's a lot like the old-time movie serials all over again.

But it's also a lot different. Soaps have managed to stay around so long because they've kept pace with the times, and changed to suit the audience.

A Taste of Silver Spoons

Edward Stratton III (Joel Higgins) was born "with a silver spoon in his mouth" — very, very rich. He had an easy, carefree childhood. In fact, Edward's childhood was so pleasant that, in some ways, he never bothered to grow up. He held on to some childlike qualities, like curiosity, openness to learning new things, and a great sense of fun.

Edward's son, Ricky (Ricky Schroder), was also born with a silver spoon in his mouth. But Ricky's childhood hasn't been so carefree. He had to learn some hard realities at an early age. Edward and Ricky's mother were divorced when Ricky was very young. Neither of his parents really knew what to do with Ricky. They put him in a military boarding school and went on with their separate lives.

Ricky hated that school so much that he ran away.

He ran to his father. After several misunderstandings, Ricky and Edward realized how much they loved each other. They recognized that they needed each other, and that they each knew things they could teach the other.

Sometimes it seems as if Ricky is the parent in the family and Edward is the son. But that's okay. The main thing is, now they're *Silver Spoons* (NBC), and they're finding their way together.

Ricky Schroder's real-life family is much larger than his *Silver Spoons* family. Ricky has over 50 first cousins! Most of them live on the East Coast. So does Ricky's dad, whose job keeps him there during the week. When *Silver Spoons* is in production, Ricky's dad flies out on weekends to join Ricky, his sister Dawn, and their mother in the family's California home. Then when Ricky has time off, he and the rest of the family fly back to their home in Connecticut.

Ricky started acting in television commercials when he was only three months old. By the time he was four years old, he'd made more than 50 commercials. His first movie was *The Champ*, with Jon Voight, when Ricky was eight. He also made the feature films *The Earthling* and *The Last Flight of Noah's Ark*. Dawn, who is also a model and an actress, was in these movies, too.

Ricky starred in *Little Lord Fauntleroy; Something So Right; There Are Two Kinds of Terrible*; and *My Life, Your Life* on TV. He's 14 years old now, and his birthday is April 13.

When *Silver Spoons* started, **Erin Gray's** role as Kate Summers was almost an afterthought. She played the wise secretary who pretty much ran Edward's toy business. (After all, *he* didn't have enough sense to do

it.) Erin played Kate so well, though, that the part grew. As Edward's girl friend and Ricky's mother-figure, she's much more involved in every episode. She has also made it necessary for Edward's character to develop more sense. Otherwise the audience might have wondered what such a terrific woman saw in him!

Erin started her career in modeling and commercials, and she still does these things. She played Colonel Wilma Deering in the *Buck Rogers in the 21st Century* series and she starred in the TV movie *Born Beautiful*. She is married and has a son named Kevan.

Even when he had to play Edward Stratton as a not-so-hot father, **Joel Higgins** did a good job. It wasn't a surprise. He'd already shown his talent for TV comedy on *Best of the West*, with Meeno Peluce.

Joel had several careers before he settled on acting. He studied advertising in college and went on to write ads. He also worked in public relations, which is related to advertising. And he was a folksinger. That's related to something he still does — writing lyrics for commercial jingles.

Joel and some friends put together their own show when they were in the Army in the late 1960s. They did their act after they were discharged, too. That led to some Broadway plays for Joel, and then television.

Aside from *Best of the West* and *Silver Spoons*, Joel was in the series *Salvage I*, with Andy Griffith. He had a role in the soap opera *Search for Tomorrow*, and he starred in the TV movies *Bare Essence*, with Genie Francis, and *Threesome*, with Stephen Collins and Deborah Raffin.

Behind the Screen: Talking Back to TV

What if you could go to school without having to leave the house? Maybe you could sleep a little later in the morning.

What if you could see your friends across town — or across the country — from your living room? It could save a lot of energy.

These things could be possible with interactive television. Combining the technologies of telephones, television, and computers might someday bring the outside world literally into your home — and let you "go out" without ever having to get wet in the rain.

If you live in Columbus, Cincinnati, Pittsburgh, Dallas, Houston, or St. Louis, and if you have cable TV, maybe you already know about interactive television. These cities have tried a TV experiment called QUBE, produced by Warner Amex. That's the company that produces Nickelodeon (a cable channel for kids) and MTV. QUBE subscribers could use a hand-held computer attached to their TV screens. The computer would let them do things like vote on the ending to a program, or give answers to survey questions.

Because interactive TV "sees" into your home almost the way you see programs, it can perform other services, too. Interactive TV has been used for shopping and banking at home. It's been hooked up to burglar alarm and fire detection systems.

Interactive TV hasn't caught on in a big way yet. One reason is that some people feel the convenience of interactive TV isn't worth the possible problems.

Being able to talk through your TV set means someone else is able to listen. The idea of strangers being able to see into our homes sounds like Big Brother in George Orwell's *1984*. Will we have to clean the house before we turn on the TV set? Who'll see the records of how we vote or what we buy through TV? What could they do with that information?

What would it be like to only see your friends or teachers through a TV screen? A little distance can be nice sometimes, but some people think modern life is too impersonal already. Would interactive TV make it worse?

Interactive TV is still a new idea that may catch on after all. There's no guarantee it will create the problems we've mentioned, but they're something to think about. New technologies can make our lives better if *people* make sure they do.

The Fall Guy Who Lands on his Feet

On television or in the movies, a "stunt" is anything that might be dangerous, or that could get a person hurt. It might be taking a punch in a fight scene. It could be "flying" in a car on *The Dukes of Hazzard* or *Knight Rider*. It might be leaping from a building in an escape scene.

Most stunts are done by specially trained stuntpeople. They wear the same costume as the actor they're doing the stunt for. The camera stays far enough away from their faces so that the audience can't tell the difference.

Stuntpeople get their names in the credits when the show is over, but they don't usually get recognized when they're walking in the street. We *might* say, "Wasn't that a terrific stunt!" But we're not likely to think about the stuntperson who performed it.

One of the things *The Fall Guy* (ABC) does is make us aware of stuntpeople. Lee Majors plays one, named Colt Seavers. The title comes from the fact that Colt "takes the fall" for the person he's substituting for when he does a stunt.

Stuntwork is hard, but Colt makes it look easy. He even has time and energy for another job — chasing bad guys across the country and solving crimes. How does Colt manage such a demanding life?

Two things help: It doesn't hurt to have assistance from helpers like Howie (Doug Barr), Terri (Markie Post), and Jodie (Heather Thomas). And it doesn't hurt to have real-life stuntpeople (like Bob Bralver and Mickey Gilbert) who plan and do the dangerous stunts on *The Fall Guy*.

Lee Majors never thought about being a stuntman when he was growing up. He didn't even think about acting. Lee was more interested in sports.

He was so good at high school football that he won a scholarship to Indiana University. Two years later, he transferred to Eastern Kentucky. A bad back injury took him out of the line-up in his third year. He coached the freshman team and got himself back in shape. The next year, he went back to playing. He wore a back brace and still did so well that the St. Louis Cardinals invited him to their football tryouts.

Lee said no. He'd made plans to teach school and be a football coach. He moved his wife and their son, Lee, Jr., to Los Angeles.

Instead of going into teaching, though, Lee went to work for the Parks and Recreation Department as an assistant playground director. He got friendly with actors who came to the park. They thought he could be a successful actor.

Now that someone mentioned it, that sounded like a great idea to Lee. He found an agent and signed up for acting lessons. The agent helped get Lee a role on the series *The Big Valley*. He went from that hit to several others — *The Man from Shiloh; Owen Marshall, Counsellor at Law; The Six Million Dollar Man*; and, now, *The Fall Guy*.

Lee's professional career has gone very well. In addition to his hit series, he's been in TV movies and feature films. He does commercials for a diet cola. His personal life has sometimes been harder. His father died before Lee was born. Lee's mother was killed by a drunk driver when Lee was only two-and-a-half. He was raised by relatives.

Lee was married to and divorced from Farrah Fawcett. She guest-starred on the pilot of *The Fall Guy*, and Lee sings about her in the show's title song.

Lee hasn't let the hard parts of his life get him down. He makes a terrific *Fall Guy* on TV, and in real life, he always seems to land on his feet.

Behind the Screen: Bloopers, Blunders, and Bleeps

Some TV programs are real mistakes. We're not talking about shows like *Just Our Luck* or *Mr. Smith*. Those series had a lot of publicity before they started. Then they quietly disappeared partway through the TV season because not enough people wanted to tune in. It wasn't a mistake to put them on in the first place. It was just an unlucky guess.

No, the mistakes we're talking about are *bloopers*. A blooper is a mistake that got caught by the camera. It's the kind of thing that in real life would make you go, "Whoops!"

The bloopers are taken out of a final production, but they aren't thrown away. Cast and crew get a good laugh looking at them when the TV season is over.

In 1981, Dick Clark got the idea that an audience might enjoy seeing some of the bloopers he had collected. Clark is a TV host and producer. He's been on *American Bandstand* since 1957. NBC also thought a show made up of bloopers might interest an audience.

Clark and NBC were right. Last season, more people watched blooper shows than watched some of the shows the bloopers came from. *TV's Censored Bloopers #6*, *TV's Greatest Censored Commercial Bloopers*, and *Life's Most Embarrassing Moments*, were all among kids' 30 favorite programs last year.

Bloopers turned out to be too popular to be limited to specials. Last spring, NBC started showing an hour-long *TV's Bloopers and Practical Jokes* series (co-hosted by Dick Clark) every week. And ABC offered a half hour of *Foul-Ups, Bleeps, and Blunders* each week. Both shows were renewed for this fall.

Sometimes blooper shows seem mean. They get us to laugh at people who are embarrassed through no fault of their own. But blooper programs also show us that you can make a mistake and still get the job done.

Behind the Screen: The People You Never See

Writers write the lines, and actors speak those lines and act them out. But what about some of those other people whose names crawl by in credits before or after a program? What do they have to do with television?

The **producer** is the person responsible for the day-to-day operations when an episode is being made. He or she may oversee casting, hire the director of photography, and work with the unions in the hiring of camera, sound, and lighting people. The producer makes decisions on the set for a show. The **executive producer** has even more responsibility, though it's slightly removed. He or she makes the final decisions about the direction of a series as a whole. The executive producer hires the actors, writers, directors, story editors, etc. A **supervising producer** makes sure that details stay consistent from one episode to the next; for instance, that we see the episode where the characters meet before we see the one where they get married.

The **director** is responsible for what we see and hear when the program comes on. Sometimes scenes are shot out of sequence. The director helps the actors keep track of where each scene will fit in the final version. He or she works with the director of photography to make sure we're looking at Gary Coleman when Gary says "Whachutalkinabout?!" on *Diff'rent*

Strokes. The director also helps actors decide how to read their lines. The director usually gets the last credit before the program starts.

The **director of photography** decides where the camera should be placed, what kind of lens should be used, and how the lights should be set up to get the look the director wants.

A **second-unit director** works on hour-long shows or movies when there are scenes that don't involve the main actors. For example, if there's a chase scene performed by stuntpeople on *Knight Rider*, the second-unit director will take a separate camera crew (the second unit) and film the scene while the director is working with David Hasselhoff. This means two scenes can be shot at one time, saving time and money.

The **art director** designs the set, is in charge of props, and chooses locations for outdoor scenes.

On a record, sometimes different instruments are recorded separately. There may be a guitar track, a drums track, and a voice track that are all put together in the end to make one final *soundtrack*. The same thing happens on TV and in the movies. Actors' lines, music, and sound effects may be recorded separately. The **sound mixer** takes all the soundtracks and puts them together in the right balance.

Writers change from episode to episode. **Story editors** generally stay with a series. The story editor works with the writer and the script. He or she helps work out an idea for an episode. The story editor also makes sure that Archangel on *Airwolf* isn't asked to say a line that fits better with Dominic's personality.

Most TV shows and movies record more pictures and sound than they need for the final production. The **editor** picks the best pictures and sound to tell the story. The editor's main job comes after the actors, camera operators, and other people on the set are finished. Editing is as important as directing, especially in movies.

The **script supervisor** in television works with a stopwatch to make sure that each scene is the right length. He or she also notes any changes made in the script after it's been handed out, and makes sure the actors get copies of line changes. If a scene is stopped in the middle, the script supervisor makes sure Mr. T has the same fist lifted when the cameras start again.

Stagehands or **grips** are the people who move the scenery. The **key grip** is the grip in charge. The **best boy** is the key grip's assistant.

Electricians or **gaffers** work with the lights. The **lighting director** or director of photography makes a basic plan for where lights will be placed during each shot or scene. Gaffers make sure the lights are in place and on or off when they're supposed to be.

Behind the Screen: How to Write to the Stars

All TV can be interactive. Sometimes you just have to use pen and paper instead of electronics.

You can write to any actor on any TV show. You can write to a program's producer. You can write to the people at stations or networks who decide which shows to put on and which ones to cancel.

You might want to tell these people how you like their show. You might want to tell them about ideas the show gave you. Or you might want to tell them if you think they're doing a good job.

Go right ahead.

Here's how to send your letter:

Put the name of the person you're writing to on the envelope. (You can get the spelling from the program's credits.) Put the name of the program on the envelope, too. Send the letter to the local station that carried the show. If you saw the program on cable TV, send the letter to your local cable franchise. The addresses are in the phone book.

If you write "Please Forward" on the outside of the envelope, it will be sent on to the office of the person it's addressed to.

If you know the program is a network show, send your letter to the network instead of the local station. All of the programs written about in this book, except *Fame* and MTV, are network shows. The networks' addresses are:

ABC
4151 Prospect Avenue
Los Angeles, California 90027

CBS
7800 Beverly Boulevard
Los Angeles, California 90036

NBC
3000 West Alameda
Burbank, California 91523

The address for *Fame* is:

MGM-TV
10202 West Washington Boulevard
Culver City, California 90230

The address for MTV is:

MTV
1211 Avenue of the Americas
New York, New York 10036

Actors get a lot of mail. They can't always answer it. But they love to hear from their fans. If you're writing to an actor, try to write a letter that doesn't require an answer. Tell the person something, instead of asking for something. Maybe you will get an answer, but don't be disappointed if you don't. You should know, too, that sometimes actors (and busy producers and network people) have other people who help them with their mail. If you write something very personal, someone else might read it.

Don't let that keep you from writing! Just think carefully about what you write — the way you think carefully about what you watch.